DEAR CHURCH
FROM A DAUGHTER ADRIFT

Anna Shumpert

BookLeaf Publishing

India | USA | UK

Dear Church, From a Daughter Adrift

© 2021 Anna Shumpert

All rights reserved.

No part of this publication may be reproduced, stored in a retrieval system, or transmitted, in any form or by any means, electronic, mechanical, photocopying, recording or otherwise, without the prior written permission of the presenters.

Anna Shumpert asserts the moral right to be identified as author of this work.

Presentation by *BookLeaf Publishing*

Web: www.bookleafpub.com

E-mail: info@bookleafpub.com

ISBN: 9789358738698

First edition 2021

This book is dedicated to my parents, Terry and Lynn, for your transparency and honesty regarding your faith when all seemed lost.

ACKNOWLEDGMENTS

I would like to gratefully acknowledge the contributions of my writing group, Plonk, for providing invaluable feedback in the preparation of this collection. I would especially like to thank Jean Yoder for being an unwavering supporter of my work and the best "hype-girl" a poet could hope to have.

I would also like to acknowledge my husband, Ryan, for his unwavering support of my writing habit and for listening to my incessant droning while completing this work.

PREFACE

I've been wrestling with my place in the Church for quite some time. Conservative Evangelicalism shaped much of my early life and yet my lived experiences as a teacher, transracial adoptive parent, and friend to marginalized people has radically shifted my understanding of how the Church could and should be reaching people on the outside. This collection of poems is both a love letter and a critique of the conservative Church.

I wrote these poems as a means to wrestle with what I believed to be contradictory messages being proclaimed by church leadership and church members. Many of the pieces are questions. Questions of purpose and theology. Questions that are meant to be pondered and poured over. Questions that I cannot answer.

These poems are written by a broken Christian, a lifelong churchgoer that can no longer reconcile the message coming from the pulpit with the treatment of people who are poor, destitute, and different. And yet, despite these things, I love this community. As a child, the Church was steadfast and wise. As a young adult, the Church was my refuge and rock when my world was crumbling. As a young mother, the Church was generous and supportive.

As I write these letters to Christ's people, I hope the Church will be reflective. Know that they are written out of love. While I may be adrift, I will continue to proudly proclaim my place as a daughter.

1. THE LINE

This is my finger

dragging

a faint line

through the grit

rubble on the road

between

Drifter   and   Apostate

2. THIRD PEW FROM THE BACK

Many a young girl

born bold and brave beneath

the Mason Dixon line

was delivered on the very same pew

that cradled her head each Sunday.

There was no doubt

she'd end up here, resting

peacefully in her mother's lap,

caressing the red velvet

cushion that would one day

absorb her tears

just as it had her mother's,

and her mother's before her.

The pew was, for most

spirited women in the south,

the only gentle, yet solid,

refuge in the Church.

3. Pig Preacher & Marilyn Monroe

They were back-row Baptists,

passing as Presbyterians. Peering over

pews littered with hymnals,

bulletins, and offering envelopes

stuffed with the interest payment

they owed God for being late

every Sunday, but damn those

Hardee's biscuits were worth

the extra buck.

Pig Preacher shuffled forward, followed

by an angel of the Lord, or so she seemed.

Platinum hair and beauty mark,

skin so pale and pure it shimmered

in the stained-glass light

Mother Mary smiled down on her:

Marilyn lookalike: Pig Preacher's wife.

How did he wrestle a ring on

an angel's finger? Was he Jacob

reincarnate, forcing God to give

him Heaven's blessing? Perhaps

he sacrificed his beauty for hers,

animal for angel, to buy her allegiance.

Was this how God worked?

Maybe.

Pig Preacher's addiction exposed to

the Body boiled resentment and fury

as red as his face, the same look he wore

on those Sundays

when the Gospel'd spit

in the Congregation's eyes.

Presbyterians knew they were

chosen; no reason to cry.

Once jealous women

found solace in Marilyn's

public shaming. Pig Preacher's

propensity for porn

spoke more about his

personal pin-up

than his own sickness.

God must have crafted

a woman for this purpose:

a sponge to soak up Adam's sin.

A few years leave her

swollen with secrets,

predestined wife of

the fallen.

4. MONOCHROMATIC

I join the chorus;

slight voices sing-shouting

"Jesus Loves the Little Children,"

as parents and grandparents look on,

smiling and gesturing encouragement.
Red, yellow, black, and

white: precious in His sight,

according to the all-white Congregation.

Color, based on my narrow perception,

must be only skin-deep.

This monochromatic church and me

know nothing

of other cultures.

I assume they must be

the same as

me.

5. White Jesus Like Me

Jesus got whiter

the day I tried on his name

like a new Sunday outfit,

all lilac and lace,

exchanged for

proud of you

you're so nice

such a good kid

compliment coins

clink clinking inside

my princess saving jar.

I counted my earnings,

then approached the altar,

seeking a trade; my change

for a crisp cotton sundress.

I'd stepped over garments spilled

onto the ground: leather-studded

jackets, black headscarves,

knitted shawls trampled by

us Bible-belt Protestants;

we only bought our version

of Sunday Best.

My choice erased any Jesus

different from me.

6. HOMELESS AND HUNGRY; ANYTHING HELPS

I graduated from the backseat of my father's sedan the same day we encountered a man at the stoplight near my house—unbathed, unshaven, with a backpack and hard lines cut into his leathery face.

His wrinkled cardboard sign read: homeless and hungry; anything helps

The coins stuck to the bottom of the crusty cupholder called my name, and I dug a few out with my fingernails, plopped them into my father's lap, and pointed at the guy holding the sign.

I could feel something stir inside my chest.

I wasn't prepared for the clink clinking sound of the coins dropping like weights back into their nest followed by a quick story involving the man, a twenty, and a paper bag as the only explanation I would get.

As he disappeared behind us, emptiness replaced all the compassion that had filled that small space.

7. SECOND TIME'S THE CHARM

Twice baptized

Infant sprinkle

Adult submersion

Reliving repentance

I must ensure I've done it right,

so I do it twice over.

8. CHRISTMAS TRADITION: A SONG

Mary did you know

a song slipping

through the lips of

a middle-aged baritone

soulfully strumming

the chords of an acoustic

guitar would make a mockery

of your blessed son's birthday?

Mary did you know

the solemn singing

each and every Christmas,

once a reminder of

your son's birth and death,

would become no more

than a symbol of the Church's

stranglehold on tradition?

Mary did you know

this song for you

would fall flat,

evoking groans from

church goers who'd lost

sight of your struggle?

Did you know

we'd weary of your story

without joining you

on the journey?

9. GIVE THANKS

A feast of turkey, rolls, and pie

Served in aluminum to-go containers

From the Good Works assembly line.

There was no way better to give thanks.

Driving dirt roads to a double-wide,

a rusty '85 Ford sitting in the drive,

a dog growling through beat-up blinds.

There was no way better to give thanks.

Together, the first time in a while,

our family delivered a meal to

a scruffy man waiting in the drive.

There was no way better to give thanks.

The Spirit moved him to generosity.

He offered us a roadkill deer swarming

With bees, the only thing he could find.

There was no way better to give thanks.

10. THE BREAD, THE BODY

Once a month,

the silver trays

crushed crackers

unsalted

supposedly the Savior

in my hands.

I remember my parents telling me to skip the ritual

the Sunday I brought a friend to church.

Once a month,

my hands clasped

communion crumbs

exalted

as prayers passed

over my lips.

I remember holding my piece longer to show everyone how serious I was about my sin.

Once a month,

grinding the pieces

flavorless flour

stuck

clinging to crevices

in my teeth.

I remember waiting and wondering why the transformation from bread to body never came.

11. FRAN

In the back row of a 15-passenger van

a blonde, 25-year-old, married woman

reached out to hold my hand.

In a hushed voice she offered

a landing spot for the anger I'd been

working to suffocate with laughter.

She was the youth pastor's wife,

and that retreat to Gatlinburg was an

escape from my faux fairytale life.

12. GOOD ENOUGH

Seventeen.

I declared

a Catholic boy

an ineligible bachelor.

He wasn't Christian

enough–

didn't know

the newest Chris Tomlin song,

hadn't gone to Passion

read *Wild at Heart.*

He couldn't possibly

be good enough for me.

13. SIGNS

Swinging softly in a hung hammock,

collecting whispers from an entity

you aren't certain you'll ever see.

Gazing across a mountain pond,

plucking thoughts of Jesus like

petals from a just-bloomed flower.

The breeze catches the water,

sends a shiver across your skin.

The pond bursts

a thousand glittering lights.

You know He's listening when

you ask Him for a sign.

14. PROOF

All of the proof I need

exists in my tear ducts

when a melody squeezes

my chest and leaves me

wondering why a God so big

would see to it that I had emotions at all.

15. INTERCESSION

An elderly secretary, now widow,

started a prayer group

at work.

A nature-loving college student

seeking a way to bond

with bros.

The Spirit imparted upon each

a gift to intercede,

to speak truth

beyond their knowledge,

bridge the gap,

heal the weak.

Sometimes I envy their ability,

but I see their burden and know

that fruit wasn't meant for me.

16. Sunday Service Coffee Bar

One day, when you are older,

the coffee bar on Sunday

will be your breakfast buffet.

You'll find excitement when

a donut or cinnamon roll, slightly stale,

finds its way onto your napkin-plate.

You'll begrudgingly sprinkle

powdered creamer in your coffee,

accept this as adulthood summed up.

17. VOLUNTOLD

The nursery on Sundays,

full of other people's

precious babes, ain't a place

I ever want to be.

Gingham baby shorts,

oversized hair bows,

white pleather shoes,

pretense in full bloom.

A tiny tots has a nose

dripping like a faucet.

Two more screaming 'cause

they're separated from mommy.

Changing diapers is a drag

on any stinky butt, even

worse when you find out

it's cloth that the kids packin'.

Yet, here I am signing up

for an hour and a half slot.

The Children's Ministry Director

caught me at drop off.

18. SISTER THEOPHANE

The Good Lord's calling

didn't erase her doubt.

Black stains beneath

her nails spill a secret

Theophane could easily hide,

as her habit hid her hair

from prying eyes.

Even a Sister couldn't love herself

the way she was made.

19. DESERT DRIFTING

This drifting state-

this wondering-

my forty-year sentence

for not believing

in goodness

in kindness

in trust

I lost track of the promise

I fell out of grace

He led me from Egypt

a captive no more

offered me freedom

which I rejected with scorn

I've held on to a truth

that was my own making

God couldn't possibly forgive

all the rules I was breaking

I strangled my faith

in a merciful savior

worshipped a judge

acknowledged only my failure

My refusal to answer

His call to acceptance

has me wondering this desert

my prolonged penance.

20. FULFILLMENT

After God formed Adam,

coaxed him unconscious,

stole a rib from his side,

created Eve,

did He already know

a woman's role?

a filter

a rag

a sponge

for Man

Adam's rage and guilt

Drips from his lips. Eve,

parched and dry,

drinks him in-

a spring of life.

She finds fulfillment

in her new purpose.

She finds feelings

in her fullness.

But she can only hold so much.

She seeps the excess.

Adam blames her

for the slow trickle,

bitterness reborn,

never noticing

it's his vile liquid

she's now leaking.

21. EL ROI

The God who sees.

I can't help but wonder

what you see when your

gaze finally shifts to me.

Do you see a woman

put together, calm,

or the mom struggling to

keep it together at all?

Your name suggests

you see us both,

outer idealist,

inner turmoil.

I pray you'll love me

equally.

22. THE GARDEN

If you were Adam

and I, Eve,

what temptation

would our Apple be?

Our teeth sink deep

into the blood-red flesh.

We know now the scope

of our insignificance.

We fail to grasp

the ruse of Rights,

false Freedoms often

divide, not unite.

The mortal touch

spoils our own Liberty;

the same Apple dangles

from that dreaded tree.

23. JUDAS

We'd all like to claim

Simon Peter or John,

preferably not Thomas,

certainly not Saul, maybe Paul.

But what if God

chose us as Judas,

born a betrayer,

acting according to

divine duty and purpose?

What if for some,

serving Country and God

become one in the same.

Could we accept a calling

that would kill our Christ

to fulfill His prophesy

if it left us spiritually

destitute with nothing

but a ruined name?

24. THE LEAST OF THESE

Dear Church,

This is your Daughter crying

out. I need help

reconciling your words

and The Word.

Your message of war

and clashing cultures

has me suiting up

instead of reaching out.

The fear drips off your tongue,

has me clinging to life like

it's about to be stolen

by some menace, some enemy.

Your conflicting communication

has me wary of every stranger

because you can't get

the Wanted sketch just right.

Do I love my neighbor

as myself, or build a fence

when he asks for help?

Should I pray over my bread

before feeding a thousand hungry

mouths, or eat my loaf by myself?

Tell me again how we are chosen,

special, a shining city on a hill,

when Jesus's views were clear:

what we did for the least of these,

we surely did for Him.

25. A PASTOR'S PAINTING

Mr. Pastor Man ain't much

for telling his congregation to

straighten up 'cept when

he's using scripture to paint

a vague picture of a sin

he would rather not name.

Mr. Pastor Man doesn't use

his pulpit to talk about

real issues like race 'cause

it's easier to paint with a

broader brush, so his

examples are extra vague.

Mr. Pastor Man lost

his flock when all the

divisive topics dividing us

became conversations

of politics instead of the

moral obligations of us all.

26. RETHINKING REPENTANCE

Dear Church,

Have you ever considered

that your hard line on sin

grows secrets and shame?

Do you believe that we can

conquer addiction by uttering

a prayer and never be the same?

Don't make repentance yet another

bullet on my long list of failures when

I inevitably must start over again.

27. ALL MEANS ALL

How long should I hide

my friends from the Church?

The transexual and liberal

and religiously diverse-

Each encounter has me questioning

what love really looks like

when we're preaching

Christ died for all but

don't really mean them.

28. A PRODIGAL ON EASTER

New dresses in pastels.

"He is Risen" signs abound.

Every Sunday service boasts

a record-breaking crowd.

For the first ever Easter,

I refuse to be found.

Prodigal Daughter.

Title Claimed.

Not Lost.

This moment with the Church

has altered my perception.

Upon serious reflection,

I can't simply cease wondering,

accept the invitation.

29. ON THE OUTSIDE

Dear Church,

What's captured your attention?

Outside of my news and Facebook

feeds, it's not often

I hear your message.

Seems we believers prefer

preaching to each other,

handing over our

calling and responsibilities

to an institution run by a man

we worship like God.

I'm not sure you'd stop

your political banter

to see my seat empty,

if not for these letters

calling you out by name.

30. BOTH

Let this page

remember

the depths and

the mountaintops

both

there is no valley

without the high.

Let this page

birth

conversation and

personal reflection

both

a conduit for

understanding.

Let this page

celebrate

the failures and

accomplishments

both

a learning experience

for all.

Let this page

serve

the believer and

non-believer

both

perfect children of

the Most High.